GOOD MANNERS IN GOD'S HOUSE

For Little Catholics

By Sister Mary Saint Paul of Maryknoll

Edited by Bart Tesoriero

ISBN: 978-1-61796-399-5

Printed in China

In the park, you play games. You shout and run and jump. This is the right way to act when you play.

You act in other ways
at home.
You act in other ways
at school.

Still, it is fun to be noisy. It is fun to play. It makes you feel good.

But you can feel good, too, when you are very, very QUIET.

Can you think of a place that is very quiet? It is a place that everyone loves. This special place is God's house. It is the church.

Every church is the palace of your King. Your King is Jesus. And Jesus is God.

Sometimes you visit Jesus, your King, in His palace. Then you act in special ways.

You remember that you are going to the palace of a great King. That is why you want to have:

a clean body,
clean clothes,
and brushed hair.

You want to be your best when you visit Jesus. He is your God and your King.

Jesus loves you very much. The door of His palace is always open. You go in softly and quietly. Near the door you find holy water. You put your fingertip in it.

You do not waste the holy water.
You make a big Sign of the Cross with it.

And you say:
"In the name of the Father, and of the Son, and of the Holy Spirit. Amen."

Now you are in the palace of the great King, our Lord Jesus Christ. He is there on the altar. He sees you walk softly down the aisle. And He watches you with love.

You are no longer just a plain child. You are a special child of God, your King. Every boy is a prince. Every girl is a princess in the Church of God.

On you go until you come to the place where you will sit. You bend your right knee before Jesus. You make sure your knee touches the floor. Then you walk all the way into the seat.

This pleases your King because He wants you to leave room for others.

You love God very much. You want many other people to come to Him, so you leave space for them. Then they will not have to crawl over you.

Sometimes everyone seems quiet in church, but everyone is talking to Jesus. They are talking a special kind of talk and Jesus can hear everyone at once. That is because He is God.

You can send messages to God from your heart. The message He likes most is: "My God, I love You."

Prayer books help you learn how to talk to God. A rosary, a crucifix, holy pictures, and statues help you to think of God.

At Mass, the priest dresses in long robes. They are like the robes that Jesus wore. You watch the priest, and this helps you to think of Jesus.

Your prayer book about the Mass will tell you what to do. You stand when Father enters and again when he leaves. And you stand up straight.

When the altar server rings the bell, you kneel up straight. Some children do this very well. Keep practicing. You will learn to do it well, too.

Babies cannot sit still very long. They are always looking this way and that.

But you are not a baby. You will not look this way and that in church. You will look straight ahead and keep your eyes on your King.

Practice the right way of acting in God's house. Teach others to act in the right way. Then God will know you are His friend. He will watch you leave the church. And He will let you take His happiness with you. He will help you to be happier than ever.

RULES FOR VISITORS TO THE KING

1. Boys take off their hats or caps in church. They tip their hats when they pass a church.
2. Girls keep their heads covered in church. They bow their heads when they pass a church.
3. Visitors to the King never chew gum or eat in church.
4. They try to be still when they sit.
5. They leave spaces between them and the people who are next to them.
6. They never play in church.
7. Their feet are side by side when they stand.
8. They put money in the collection. This helps to keep God's palace beautiful. Sometimes the collection helps the poor.
9. They pray that the entire world will know and love its great King.